WAR PLANES

Air Superiority Fighters:
The F/A-22 Raptors
by Michael and Gladys Green

CAPSTONE
HIGH-INTEREST
BOOKS

an imprint of Capstone Press
Mankato, Minnesota

Capstone High-Interest Books are published by Capstone Press
151 Good Counsel Drive, P.O. Box 669, Mankato, Minnesota 56002
http://www.capstone-press.com

Library of Congress Cataloging-in-Publication Data
Green, Michael, 1952-
　　Air superiority fighters: F/A-22 Raptors /by Michael and Gladys Green.
　　p. cm.—(War planes)
　　Summary: Discusses the design and weapons of the F/A-22 Raptor fighter jet (formerly called the F-22) and how it is used by the Air Force.
　　Includes bibliographical references and index.
　　ISBN 0-7368-2148-1 (hardcover)
　　1. F-22 (Jet fighter plane)—Juvenile literature. [1. F-22 (Jet fighter plane)
2. Fighter planes. 3. Airplanes, Military.] I. Green, Gladys, 1954- II. Title. III. Series.
UG1242.F5G7124 2004
623.7'464—dc21　　　　　　　　　　　　　　　　　　　　2003000079

Editorial Credits
Christine Peterson, editor; Timothy Halldin, series designer; Patrick Dentinger, book
　　designer; Jo Miller, photo researcher; Eric Kudalis, product planning editor

Photo Credits
All photographs courtesy of Lockheed Martin Aeronautics Company

Consultant:
Raymond L. Puffer, Ph.D., Historian, Air Force Flight Test Center, Edwards Air
Force Base, California

Table of Contents

Chapter 1 The F/A-22 in Action 5

Chapter 2 Inside the F/A-22 11

Chapter 3 Weapons and Tactics 19

Chapter 4 The Future 27

Features

Specifications 15

Photo Diagram 16

Words to Know.. 30

To Learn More 31

Useful Addresses 31

Internet Sites 32

Index 32

Chapter One

Learn About

- The F/A-22's mission
- F/A-22 development
- Test flights

The F/A-22 in Action

U.S. Air Force F/A-22 Raptor fighters are on a mission over an enemy country. Radar screens show the pilots that 25 enemy planes are 100 miles (161 kilometers) away.

The U.S. pilots aim their F/A-22s toward the enemy planes. The enemy's radar system does not find the F/A-22s. The F/A-22 has features that make it nearly invisible to radar. The enemy planes are now 30 miles (48 kilometers) away. The F/A-22 pilots fire their missiles at the enemy planes.

The enemy pilots do not see the approaching missiles. The missiles strike the enemy planes. Eight enemy fighters explode in the air. The U.S. pilots fire more missiles. Four more enemy planes turn into fireballs.

Enemy radar systems on the ground now spot the four F/A-22s. A dozen missiles are fired at the American planes. The enemy missiles soar into the sky. F/A-22 pilots fly their planes faster and higher. The enemy missiles can not reach the F/A-22s and explode in the air.

A Better Jet Fighter

In 1974, the Air Force got its first batch of F-15 jet fighters. The F-15 became a top fighter plane and is still in Air Force service. But Air Force officials decided a new plane would be needed.

The Air Force had many reasons to build a better fighter jet. Other countries were building new planes. Air Force leaders believed the new planes could be better than the F-15.

The F/A-22 is the Air Force's newest stealth fighter.

Foreign countries also were working on new surface-to-air missiles (SAMs). These missiles could hit planes flying at almost any altitude. The F-15 could not reach an altitude high enough to avoid these new SAMs. In 1981, the Air Force began plans for a new fighter jet.

The Testing Process

Over the next 10 years, Air Force officials looked at many designs for the new plane. In 1991, the Air Force chose a design by the Lockheed Martin Aeronautics Company for its new jet. The Boeing Company also helped design and build the new plane.

The first test flight of the new fighter took place on September 7, 1997. The new jets were named the F-22 Raptors. The plane's name was changed to the F/A-22 in 2002. The new name shows the F/A-22's skills as a fighter and attack plane.

Nine test planes were built. Pilots flew the first three F/A-22 test planes to check the jet's engines and to see how safely the plane flew. The other test planes were used to check the computers and sensors. Crews also wanted to see how well the jet could fight. Pilots took the test planes on more than 2,700 flights.

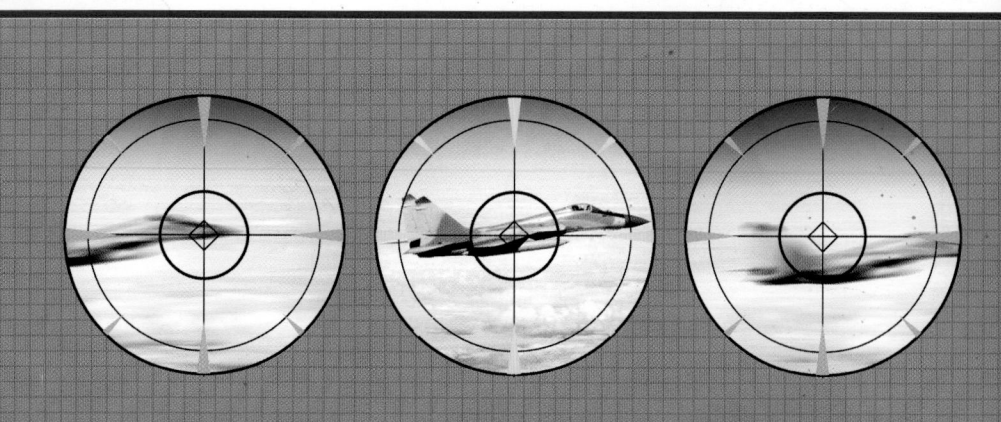

The F/A-22 has taken more than 2,700 test flights.

Learn About

- F/A-22 engines
- F/A-22 sensors
- Stealth features

Inside the F/A-22

The F/A-22 is both a supercomputer and combat fighter. The F/A-22 can fly farther and faster than any other fighter jet in service today.

Engines

The F/A-22 uses two Pratt & Whitney F119-PW-100 jet engines. Each engine can produce 35,000 pounds (15,876 kilograms) of thrust. Thrust is the force that pushes a jet forward.

The F/A-22 has a top speed of 1,500 miles (2,414 kilometers) per hour when carrying weapons. This is called supersonic speed.

Most jet planes use an afterburner to reach supersonic speed. An afterburner injects fuel at the engine's exhaust. The F/A-22's engines do not need an afterburner to reach this speed.

Most war planes can fly at supersonic speed for only a short time. The F/A-22 can fly at supersonic speed for more than one hour. The Air Force calls this ability "supercruise."

The Cockpit

The F/A-22 is a single-seat fighter jet. A clear plastic canopy covers the cockpit. The pilot can see all sides of the plane through the canopy.

The F/A-22's main controls are the throttle and control stick. The throttle controls the plane's speed. F/A-22 pilots also use the throttle to fire missiles. The control stick steers the plane. The pilot can fire the plane's automatic cannon with the control stick.

The pilot uses a head-up display (HUD) to watch the plane's gauges. The HUD is a small screen in front of the pilot. It shows the plane's speed and altitude.

Lt. Col. "Doc" Nelson

Pilots get a clear view of the plane from the cockpit.

Sensors

The F/A-22 has several electronic sensors. The sensors are connected to the plane's computer. F/A-22 pilots use data from the sensors to find enemy planes.

The F/A-22 also has an electronic warfare (EW) system and data link. These systems help F/A-22 pilots find enemy forces that are farther away.

The F/A-22 also has an advanced radar system called the APG-77. This system can find enemy planes very quickly. The APG-77 shows what kind of enemy planes are in the area.

Stealth

The F/A-22 has stealth abilities. Stealth features allow the F/A-22 to sneak past enemy sensors. These sensors include radar, heat-seeking missiles, and sound detectors.

The F/A-22's body is designed so that radar waves bounce off the plane. Radar sends powerful radio waves through the air to find planes. The F/A-22 scatters radar waves in different directions. Radar systems can only pick up small amounts of energy from the jet. Enemy forces could mistake the small amount of radar waves for a bird. Enemy radar systems may not even be able to find the F/A-22 at all.

F/A-22 Specifications

Function:	Fighter and attack
Manufacturer:	Lockheed Martin/Boeing
First Flight:	September 7, 1997
Length:	62 feet, 1 inch (18.9 meters)
Height:	6 feet, 5 inches (2 meters)
Wingspan:	44 feet, 6 inches (13.6 meters)
Engine:	Two Pratt & Whitney F119-PW-100 jet engines
Thrust:	35,000 pounds (15,876 kilograms) per engine
Speed:	1,500 miles (2,414 kilometers) per hour maximum
Ceiling:	50,000 feet (15,240 meters) maximum
Range:	1,865 miles (3,001 kilometers); (unlimited with in-flight refueling)

Parts of the F/A-22 are covered with a material that soaks up radar waves like a sponge. This feature makes it hard for radar systems to find the F/A-22.

The F/A-22 has other stealth features. The plane has heat-resistant tiles around its engine exhaust nozzles. The tiles stop heat-seeking missiles from finding the F/A-22.

nose

cockpit

The F/A-22 Raptor

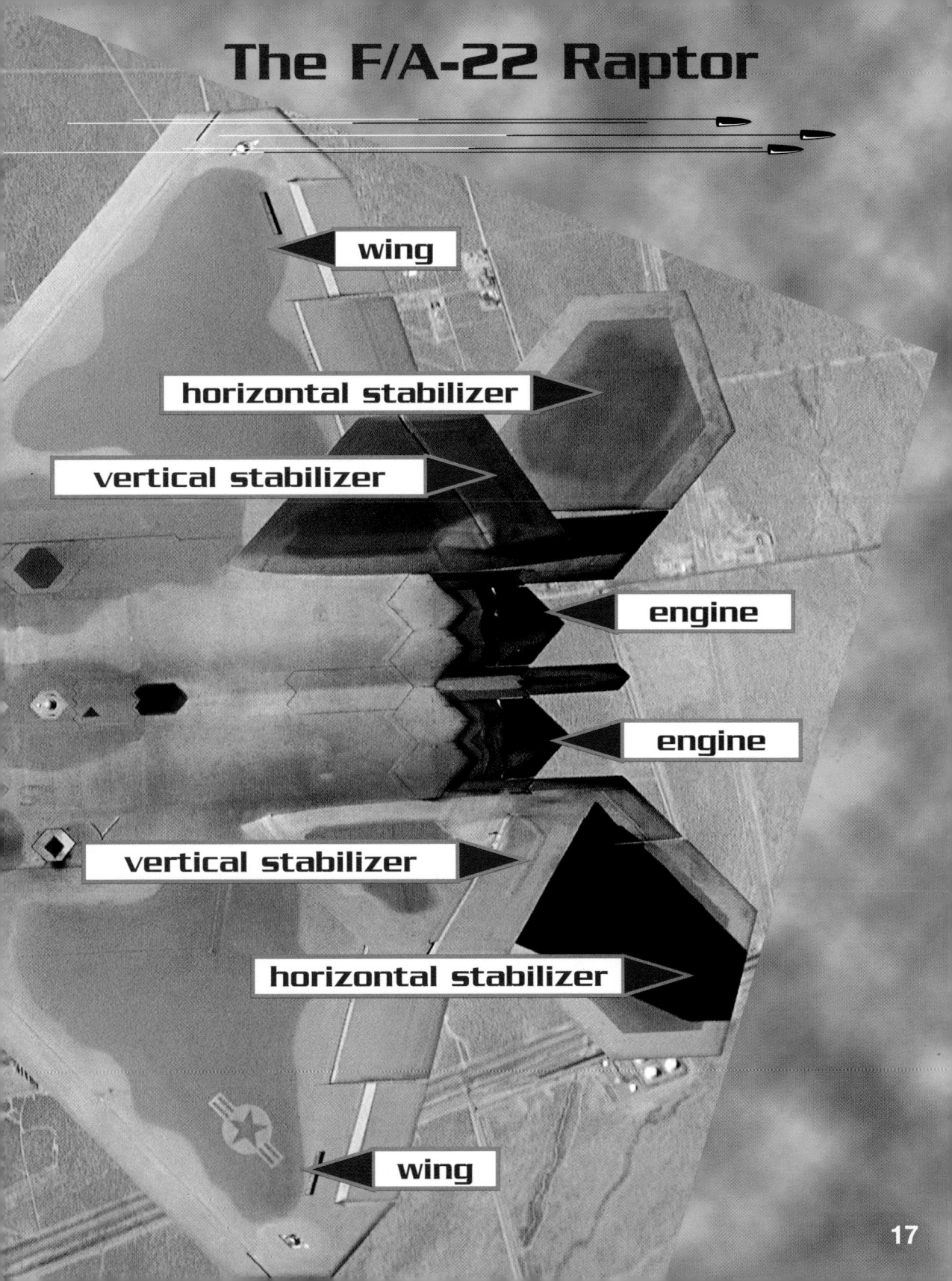

wing

horizontal stabilizer

vertical stabilizer

engine

engine

vertical stabilizer

horizontal stabilizer

wing

Chapter Three

Learn About

- F/A-22 missiles
- Smart bombs
- Weapons bays

Weapons and Tactics

The F/A-22's main job is to shoot down enemy planes. F/A-22 pilots can use two types of missiles during air-to-air combat. One missile is made to hit targets at shorter distances. The other missile is used to hit targets that are farther away.

If needed, F/A-22 pilots can use the plane's internal automatic cannon to fire at targets that are 1 mile (1.6 kilometers) away. F/A-22 pilots also drop bombs to attack enemy targets on the ground.

Air-to-Air Missiles

Guided air-to-air missiles are the most important weapons on the F/A-22. Pilots use them to shoot down other aircraft.

The F/A-22 carries eight air-to-air missiles. Two of the missiles follow the heat given off by the enemy plane. The other six missiles use radar to find their targets.

The F/A-22's heat-seeking guided missile is the AIM-9X Sidewinder. This missile is 9 feet, 5 inches (2.9 meters) long and weighs 191 pounds (87 kilograms). The AIM-9X packs a 20-pound (9-kilogram) warhead that can reach targets up to 10 miles (16 kilometers) away.

The AIM-9X has a heat-seeking sensor in its nose. The sensor aims the missile at the heat from an enemy plane's exhaust. The missile follows this heat to the target.

The F/A-22 pilot also can use the AIM-120C Advanced Medium Range Air-to-Air Missile (AMRAAM). The AIM-120C is 12 feet (3.7 meters) long and weighs 345 pounds (156 kilograms).

The F/A-22 pilot tests an air-to-air missile.

The AMRAAM's 48-pound (22-kilogram) warhead can strike targets up to 30 miles (48 kilometers) away.

Pilots can use the F/A-22's high-speed abilities during combat. Pilots may fire all of the plane's weapons in combat. Then they can quickly return the F/A-22 to base and reload.

Automatic Cannon

F/A-22 pilots have one last weapon to use if enemy planes get past the Raptor's missiles. The M61A2 automatic cannon can fire at targets less than 1 mile (1.6 kilometers) away. Pilots also can fire the M61A2 at targets on the ground.

The M61A2 has six moving barrels that can fire 6,000 rounds per minute. Since the gun barrels spin, they do not get too hot when fired. Only 480 rounds of ammunition are carried on the F/A-22. Pilots have to fire the gun in short bursts to save bullets.

Smart Bombs

The F/A-22 can carry two GBU-32 Joint Direct Attack Munitions (JDAMs). Each JDAM weighs 1,000 pounds (454 kilograms). The JDAM is called a smart bomb because it uses data from satellites to find targets.

The F/A-22's weapons bays only open to fire weapons.

The JDAM uses information from sensors inside a tail guidance kit. This kit is placed on back of a plain bomb. The sensors inside the kit turn a plain bomb into a smart bomb.

The F/A-22's weapons are hidden inside the plane.

The JDAM is programmed with the target's exact location. Pilots then fire the JDAM when the plane is about 15 miles (24 kilometers) away from the target. Information from the satellites guides the missile to its target. If needed, the F/A-22 pilots can change the JDAM's target after the missile has been fired.

Internal Weapons Bays

All weapons on the F/A-22 are stored inside the plane. The internal weapons bays help to hide the F/A-22 from enemy radar systems. By storing weapons inside the plane, the F/A-22 uses less fuel. The F/A-22 can then fly farther than other planes.

Other planes carry weapons on the outside of their frames. The weapons produce drag which makes a plane burn more fuel. Weapons carried outside the plane also are easy to find by radar.

There are three weapons bays inside the F/A-22. Doors cover the weapons bays. The doors open when weapons are fired.

Pilots may add extra weapons or fuel tanks to the outside of the plane after enemy radar systems have been destroyed. The F/A-22 does not need to refuel as often when carrying extra fuel tanks.

Chapter Four

Learn About

- F/A-22 deployment
- F/A-22 cost
- The need for the F/A-22

The Future

F/A-22 pilots will complete many hours of training before taking the Raptor into combat. The Air Force plans to have at least three groups of F/A-22s ready for combat in 2008. These groups will have a total of 78 planes. Production of the F/A-22 should be completed in 2013.

High Price Tag

The F/A-22 has cost a great deal of money to plan and build. In 2002, the total cost for the F/A-22 program was more than $60 billion.

Each F/A-22 costs about $99 million. The Raptor costs about 25 percent more to build than other military planes. The Air Force plans to buy about 300 F/A-22s.

The Need

People disagree about the F/A-22. Some people think the Air Force does not need the F/A-22. They say the Air Force should use the F-35A Joint Strike Fighter that costs less to build. The Air Force plans to put the F-35A in service in 2010.

The Air Force says the F-35A is being made to attack ground targets. The F-35A is not meant to serve as a fighter plane. The Air Force says the F/A-22 would be a strong plane in air-to-air combat.

The Air Force saw the need for an advanced fighter jet more than 20 years ago. The F/A-22 combines speed and stealth to attack enemy targets. These abilities will make the F/A-22 a jet fighter for the future.

Lockheed Martin will build about 300 F/A-22 Raptors.

Words to Know

drag (DRAG)—the force created when air hits a moving object; drag slows down the object.

exhaust (eg-ZAWST)—heated air leaving a jet engine

radar (RAY-dar)—equipment that uses radio waves to locate and guide objects

sensor (SEN-sur)—an instrument that detects physical changes in the environment

smart bomb (SMART BOM)—a bomb that can be aimed as it moves toward enemy targets

stealth (STELTH)—a plane's ability to fly secretly

supersonic (soo-pur-SON-ik)—faster than the speed of sound

throttle (THROT-uhl)—a control on an airplane that allows pilots to increase or decrease the plane's speed

thrust (THRUHST)—the force created by a jet engine; thrust pushes an airplane forward.

warhead (WOR-hed)—the part of a missile that carries explosives

To Learn More

Berliner, Don. *Stealth Fighters and Bombers.* Aircraft. Berkeley Heights, N.J.: Enslow, 2001.

Chant, Christopher. *Role of the Fighter and Bomber.* The World's Greatest Aircraft. Philadelphia: Chelsea House, 2000.

Maynard, Christopher. *Aircraft.* The Need for Speed. Minneapolis: Lerner, 1999.

Useful Addresses

Air Force Flight Test Center
Public Affairs Office
1 South Rosamond Boulevard
Edwards AFB, CA 93524

United States Air Force Museum
1100 Spaatz Street
Wright-Patterson AFB, OH 45433

Internet Sites

Do you want to find out more about the F/A-22 Raptors? Let FactHound, our fact-finding hound dog, do the research for you.

Here's how:
1) Go to *http://www.facthound.com*
2) Type in the **Book ID** number: **0736821481**
3) Click on **FETCH IT**.

FactHound will fetch Internet sites picked by our editors just for you!

Index

afterburner, 12
AIM-120C, 20
AIM-9X Sidewinder, 20
APG-77, 14

Boeing, 8

cockpit, 12

data link, 13

engines, 11, 12
electronic warfare
    system, 13

F-15, 6–7
F-35A, 28

heat-resistant tiles, 15
HUD, 12

JDAM, 22–23, 25

Lockheed Martin, 8

M61A2 cannon, 22

SAMs, 7
stealth, 14–15
supercruise, 12
supersonic speed, 12

weapons bays, 25